Praise for Boyd Bauman:

"An old cliché talks about how a reader does not need to leave her/his chair to travel the world. In his collection of poetry *Scheherazade Plays the Chestnut Tree Cafe*, Boyd Bauman's poems convert the chair into a TARDIS to whisk us away into his examinations of world travels. Alongside these, Bauman shows us his rural Kansas upbringing, too, and the times of unknowing in the midst of organized religion and ranch-talk. He lends a lens to the racism of that childhood world: *though we didn't have a clue / who a queer was / and what would a black man / want with a town like ours...* Through these complications examined in this work, we get to see the worlds we know, the worlds that need revealed, and the worlds we haven't visited but understand what we do is to survive, just as Bauman shares with us through looking at Iceland's poet Egil: *Poets are forged / simply by bearing witness / to the nature of this land, / this land of temper / and skáld (other poets)."*

-Dennis Etzel, Jr., author of *This Removed Utopia*

"Here is work by a poet who writes with intelligence, understanding and remarkable wisdom, a gift that makes his poetry a joy to read. He reaches into his past to share indelible memories of a life spent in rural Kansas and much of the rest of the world. His tough and pertinent evaluation of religious life in America is spot-on—folks who have created a god in their own image. His tendency to formalism is delightful. Here's just a sample. There are so many more. Bauman's poem, "Stockyards" morphs into an ode near the end: *Oh, Chicago/hog butcher of the world,/ has your past dissolved like my memory . . . ?* And in the poem, "Communion", a well-deserved jab at athletes and sports fans who actually believe that God cares who wins a competition: *not only the one true path to His Kingdom, /but also define right to victory /in the sanctuary of home court.*"

-H.C. Palmer, 2017 Balcones Poetry Prize finalist and Kansas Notable Book Award winner for *Feet of the Messenger*

Scheherazade Plays the Chesnut Tree Cafe

Poems by Boyd Bauman

Kansas City   Missouri

Spartan Press
Kansas City, MO
spartanpresskc@gmail.com

Copyright © Boyd Bauman, 2019
First Edition 1 3 5 7 9 10 8 6 4 2
ISBN: 978-1-950380-04-6
LCCN: 2019932566

Design, edits and layout: Jason Ryberg
Cover art by Alejandro Sandoval-Espinoza (alesanesp99@gmail.com).
Title page image: Haven Bauman
Author photo: Stephen Aspleaf
All rights reserved. No part of this publication may be reproduced or transmitted in any form or by any means, electronic or mechanical, including photocopying, recording or by info retrieval system, without prior written permission from the author.

The author thanks Jason Ryberg, Walter Bargen, Dennis Etzel,Jr., H.C. Palmer, Alejandro Sandoval-Espinoza, and Haven Bauman.

Special thanks to the editors of the following publications where some of *Scheherazade Plays the Chestnut Tree Cafe*'s poems first appeared, sometimes in slightly different form:

The Flint Hills Review: "Lava Soap Dirge"
Nomad's Choir: "Talking About the Weather"
Plainsongs: "Graveyard in Passing," "Relative Cold Front"
The Konza Poetry Project Presents; Somewhere Between Kansas City and Denver: "Spring Eternal," "Lava Soap Dirge" and "Recipe for Making a Delicacy of Spam"

"Smear the queer" is partially inspired by a Ross Gay poem of the same title.

CONTENTS

Quang, PhD / 1

Spring Eternal / 4

Iceland / 6

Lava Soap Dirge / 8

Good Steward / 10

Recipe for Making a Delicacy of Spam / 12

Baptism of the Dead / 14

Twist of Fate / 16

Ode to the Peanut / 17

Beanstalk, Revisited / 19

Rashomon / 22

Narcissus takes a selfie / 24

Sweet Here, After / 26

Ode to Blockbuster / 27

Homeschooled / 29

Smear the queer / 31

Queue / 33

Conversion / 35

Scope / 37

The ice cream man drives way too fast
    down my street / 38

Asian Markets / 40

Sum of Our Parts / 42

Faith by Works / 43

Grade Inflation / 45

The Mendoza Line / 47

Cottonwood / 49

Nondenominational / 51

Flint Hills / 53

Friends of the Truth / 54

Irony / 58

Cold Case / 60

Parochial Praise / 61

Slough / 63

Relative Cold Front / 64

Angels and Devils / 66

Best case scenario / 67

Stockyards / 69

Graveyard in Passing / 71

Diaspora / 73

House of Cards / 74

Danse Macabre / 76

Parent-Teacher Conferences / 78

Forgiving Eve / 80

Aunt Priscilla / 81

Parental Prayer / 83

Communion / 84

Talking About the Weather / 86

To Joe: Thanks for the stories.

Quang, PhD

Saigon

One sings the first syllable   Sai
Again
The note lifts as the bird takes wing   Sai
Better

The second syllable invoked, summoned
Cao Dai monks
fathoming deeper truth   gon

                                          gon

          Sai   gon

Saigon
from the back of a motorbike
The only way to see the Paris of the East
through a
                wine-besotted lens
                the bars of an old French waltz
                and the brilliantly sad eyes of Mr.

Quang   who knew where to find the best
Chinese meal in town

Keys to a happy life:
Live in a French house
Eat Chinese food
Marry a Japanese woman

Quang　　　　whose favorite restaurant kept bottles
of top shelf Italian wine
in stock　　　just for him
and served the soup that wouldn't send his ulcers spiraling

awaken the dragon in my belly

Quang　　　　who learned GI English
working with the Yanks until '75

Quang　　　　who discovered reeducation
in the middle of life　　　at the end of promise
who knew the texture of human feces
as he stood in shit
and broke up by hand the bigger clumps to fertilize crops
in the camp of former boys

Quang　　　　who had a piece of mango
placed in his mouth
by a comrade　　　while knee deep in his labors
the sweetest fruit he had ever tasted
　　　　　　　　like a drop of the sun on my tongue
　　　　　　　　I swallowed it with the reverence
　　　　　　　　of my first communion

Quang   who knew sacrifice meant
sending a family away
from a father's crippled prospects
and what it meant to be a foreigner
in the eyes of his children

> *I tell ya, buddy*
> *I've got a PhD in life*

Quang   who knew the perfect spot to pause
and cut the motorbike's engine
to catch the moon's reflection
in the ripples of the Song Saigon
who knew to linger only until
memories begin flooding the banks

Quang   who knew every verse to "Que Sera, Sera"
by heart
> *Whatever will be, will be*

to begin the song as a measured, vibrant waltz
then slow to melancholy requiem

to mind the pacing so
some larger truth could register
perhaps, in hopeful dirge,
from the ashes take wing.

Spring Eternal

*Some people need
more churchin' than others*
Dad proselytized
most Sunday mornings
as Mom readied herself
for the Methodist service.
Those rare Sabbaths
his tactic's success
garnered grace for the son
I was off
tin canteen in hand
bivouacking through timber,
pasture and creek
before bursting from the cornfield
to stand at the edge
of our family's spring.

Hallowed be thy name
of my father
and my father's father
for the faith
they mustered
in each seed
and the work of this earth
which brings it to light.

Love thy neighbor
as thyself
as they did
in the dust dry thirties,
filling barrels in the back
of horse-drawn wagons
for farmers to haul
to thirsty cattle and kids.

Upon this rock
I will build my church
for that was where
it was most pure,
I prostrated myself
and drank
in some depth of remembrance
the transubstantiation
of the generations
and it filled me
with as much of the eternal
as I needed to know.

Iceland

Poetry saved Egil's life
twice.
The night before his execution
was spent composing a poem
so life affirming,
King Eirik felt justice lay only
in the sparing of such a vessel.

Then again upon the death
of his son,
Egil entombed himself
in his anguish,
surfacing finally with a prayer
of thanks to the gods
for the least of abilities
to turn raw suffering to rhyme.

Misshapen Egil,
hunchbacked outcast,
cold as ice
with his Viking blade,
yet the verse
was the fire,
the volatile heart,
the muse that scalds
for skáld is Icelandic for poet

in this land of fire and ice
where fields smoke and bubble
like Shakespeare's cauldrons,
where stones ignite, spew,
congeal to truth
and ash,
where winter solstice so deep
welcomes each explorer
into the depths
of inner life,
journey to the center.
Poets are forged
simply by bearing witness
to the nature of this land,
this land of temper
and skáld.

Lava Soap Dirge

Pumice stone.
Cat's tongue.
Salt lick.
Steel file.
#40 sandpaper.
The laborer's loofah.
Rough lover of no foreplay,
you got right down
to the nitty-gritty.

As pall bearers,
distant brethren stand
on Walmart shelves erect
overcompensating -
pledging to warm, moisturize, sooth,
douche, calm, smooth, sexualize
via herb, fragrance, aroma therapy,
pH balance.

You must have dissolved
with the last real cowboy I knew.
The day's dirt smiled
under his fingernails
as he greeted you
with a man's handshake
before an epic battle erupted:

elbow grease vs. combine grease,
volcanic suds unearthing
manure,
alfalfa flecks,
WD-40,
tributaries oozing toward the drain
in molten flow
to lie somewhere dormant

save for those rare occurrences
composite of my muscle memory activates
and my hands are soiled
in honest labor,
then from my core
coagulants threaten to surface and spew
and I would sacrifice all that is pure and good
to be baptized again
in your healing abrade.

Good Steward

At the Christian family guest ranch,
my nightly charge
was to set the skunk trap
next to the trash shed.

Eye for an eye,
one got the jump on me once
on my way to the bunkhouse,
and he was spirit of my flesh
with every hard day's sweat
for the next month

which admittedly lightened the cross I bore
each morning
when placing the occupied vessel
on the tail end of the pick up
before hauling it down the valley
to the banks of Chalk Creek
where by immersion I'd baptize.

Two verses of "Amazing Grace"
was typically all it took
for the congregation to stop kicking
'Twas grace that taught my heart to fear...
body released to the current,

no soul to the other side
before I ascended the mount,
secure as a young man can be
in his black and white role
as good steward of the earth
under the porches
of our wealthy Texan guests
who slept the sleep of the just
while I affirmed our faith
in the gospel of prosperity.

Recipe for Making a Delicacy of Spam

Step One: Unseason yourself to a naive
twentysomething.

Step Two: Pour some savings
into a flight to Juneau.
Mix in a ferry ride to Sitka.

Step Three: Increase the employment rolls
of Sitka Sound Seafoods.
Stir in some revulsion
at standing on the slime line
ankle deep in fish intestine.
Add more than a pinch of pain
when promoted to the freezer crew.

Step Four: Garnish every two hours
with a measure of mercy
via a 15-minute break.

Step Five: Scoop plain white rice
onto a paper plate each break
for the first three weeks.

Step Six: Sprinkle some salt on top
the fourth and fifth week.
Simmer.

Step Seven: Splash on some soy sauce.
See how that sets
for a couple more weeks.

Step Eight: Splurge on a container
of the best Spam
your money can buy.
Spread generously.

Voila! A dollop of denial
is man's most savory
of appetizers.

Baptism of the Dead

Answer the knock
and christen me Mormon when I die.
Remember, my love, should I whisper
the long goodbye.

Let me be not skeptical as the orthodox
so proud of their monogamy,
let's say I'll go out like a Buddhist
disinclined to disturb the harmony.

I regret I gave up choir
sophomore year for shop's easy A,
and this time I'll take spring break mission trips,
not squander youth in sand, sun and play.

I can be a disciplined role player
for slow-twitch muscles atone
by perfecting a pretty pick and roll
with guidance from Stockton, Malone.

Marriage made me a responsible man,
with less ego and better health.
Let's multiply this by five and utterly
learn to relinquish self.

Though agnostic family planning
limited my earthly progeny,
I'll leave them access to a massive genealogy database,
exquisite tabernacle artistry,

and firm knowledge that after a life
of fits and starts,
their papa is finally a fraction of a sum
far greater than his parts.

Twist of Fate

Why the maneuver
as those it affects
know fate's not adverse
to being direct?

It's the lack of culpability
such a contort has got,
diplomatic immunity
for those tied in knots.

Ode to the Peanut

Cheers, you packets of honey roasted
with Smirnoff Minis offering oral
fixes to smokers of yore
on long overseas flights.

A toast to our politicians united
citizens and super
PACs removed
from the peanut farm.

Prost to our nights at Monk's Pub
under the 'L' in the Loop
casting our shells with our philosophies
to the floor in swinish intoxication.

When did you become public enemy #1?
Nut free zones plastered
down the halls of elementary schools,
pledging more permanence
than any no gun zone
soon to be legislated away.

What level of terror alert
if I forget and slip
a PB & J into my daughter's

Hello Kitty lunchbox?
Where the studies to determine
if it's the legume's first world mix
with methylphenidate and SSRIs
that produces a lethal cocktail?

Oh, George Washington Carver,
in your race to succeed,
you forgot to add a sacred amendment,
a powerful lobby to demand subsidies,
some sweet deal requiring peanut oil
in every product on the shelves.

Poor Mr. Peanut,
our one percenter,
unmonocled,
tapped out and fallen
from grace.

Beanstalk, Revisited

After perusing the government reports,
Jack's mom panics and pleads,
Son, get some traction, you must take action.
There's cuts a comin' to our subsidies!

Jack halters up the trusty cow,
goes searching for the ol' livestock exchange.
Cold callin' ain't a good plan, says the cattle man,
Now I've appointments to rearrange.

We send out a representative
once we know a feedlot is teeming
and if we test excrement, would it register top supplements?
Your bovine's so scrawny-seeming.

But you caught me on a good day.
Tell you what I'm gonna do:
Three beans to sow, endowed with the magic of GMO
should be plenty to see you through.

What if I want to diversify?
Rotation is good for the soil.
I won't leave you flat - this strain supersedes that.
Forget all that worry and toil.

Needless to say, Jack's mom is not pleased.
Laze and greed make you easy to lobby.
Gentleman farmer, she mocks, as she sits and she rocks,
Find yourself some new kind of hobby.

The stalk, as advertised, grows up overnight.
Jack climbs it in next to no time,
glimpses glitz and the glow of the 1% show,
falls into a lifestyle of crime.

Once, twice, Jack gets away.
Hubris brings him back to the scene.
Then from the giant a bellow, like not too nice a fellow,
Now, little man, you'll come clean!

The brute gives chase, Jack fears for his life.
Is it from me his hunger's to be sated?
I'm a wafer! Jack pleads, as he drops to his knees.
I'd barely taste transubstantiated!

For heaven's sake, my mind's on litigation,
says the giant as he holds the stalk steady.
Do you think I'm uncouth? I'll show you the proof:
My team of lawyers at the ready.

The fowl? The lyre? I'll give it all back!
Says the giant, *This hen's not the best.*
I've waves more in dark sheds, like in some sea beds,
steroid-buoyed by life preserver breasts.

*Long ago, this one got into the light
free ranging about on my floor,
No harm in your rustling, she's developed leg muscling.
She's no good to me anymore.*

*As for the lyre, it's a streaming device.
Everyone shares one of those.
It'll groove, it'll jive, though to hear it play live,
you'll pay for it through the nose.*

*No, in your possession is something
like religion it brings hope and joy.
Speaking plain, it's enlargin' our net profit margin.
You're messing with the sacred, my boy.*

*One's influence has to be nurtured.
Our representatives, see, they've got needs.
Now you, so obnoxious, like a thistle weed noxious,
flaunting your farm saved seeds.*

*As a card-carrying member, I could stand my ground.
Be careful lest you rage or you balk.
It's my crop, you rube, in my lab's the test tube.
He who patents the bean owns the stalk.*

Rashomon

wretched tale of
abuse
of every privilege ever
granted
he made appeal to his better
nature
or nurtured a grudge
atoning for
sins
of the father overcoming
the odds stacked
in his favor
dice so
loaded
with potential shattering
the glass
ceiling
floored by boot strap
delusions born
on third base after
a triple
threat
a matter of
perspective inspiration
arriving via a
muse

ment of the gods
' torture
authored by
his own worst enemy
was himself rejecting
belief in a
divinity shaping
his rough hewn
ends
a cyclical tale of a
ruse
of every privilege never

Narcissus takes a selfie

but upon reflection,
lines framing his fair face
are far more highly defined
than he had ever pictured.

From the depths of his soul,
he can't fathom
how the light can be so unflattering

so he freely takes
a series of shots
each captured in a cloud
of dark uncertainty
before impulsively settling
on one he loves
but isn't *in love* with

thus the instant of posting
prompts a double take.
Is that a shadow of doubt
developing under the eyes?

For the first time he shies
from the glare
for fear of a ripple effect

of an unfavorable review
impossible to skip
or, worse, an undeniable swell
of disinterest,

the pressure of which bends
his knees
to the shifting shoreline
above a reedy whisper,
an echo
of the image he once held
of himself.

Sweet Here, After

A crow trinity is in heated
theological debate
across the fence from the cemetery
of St. Ignatius Church
by the banks of Lake Michigan.

Founded in 1741 for love
of Kingdom
at Half Way on the Odawa Indian Trail,
here the Jesuits offered heathen spirits
a glorious God be with ye
to their wanderings
through the tunnel
of crooked trees.

Then why this cacophonous hymn
from the other side
as if a matter of death and life?
Iridescent rage
at being rendered obsolete
when the new believers traded
for a one way ticket?
This discordant *Why?*
Why?
Why can't we meet again
on this beautiful shore?

Ode to Blockbuster

12 blocks away.
Hand in hand from my girlfriend's house,
we'd stroll on date night Fridays,
adventure and romance
stretched before us
as far as we could see.

We progressed to hands
on a stroller handle,
adding a bit of drama,
then to additional hands
on bike and scooter handles
and plenty of action
corralling our leading ladies
down the kids' aisles,
still hopeful for a fantasy for us
after bedtimes.

12 blocks
busting with anticipation,
gratification delayed
just enough
in proportion to the joy
of acquisition.

The marquee's blue
and yellow glow
always our north star.

The greatest journeys
culminated with the one video
upon which we had staked our hopes
out of stock,
cardboard facades queued in gauntlet
to taunt us with what could have been.
Oh, the sweet disappointment!
The essential happiness of *not* having,
the voyage home with our second tactile choice
and the wild anticipation of the next epic quest.

Homeschooled,

so he learned family values:

psychology
of us vs. them,
biology
of the natural selection
of his strain
from the herd.

Gender studies with mom
taught subjugation of the weaker sex,
acceptance of the Father's wrath.

From big brother,
the geometry
of a stash configured
in the smallest containers possible,
victory of a quickly rewritten
browser history.

Religious instruction means
to an end, meanness meaningless
if one is faithful to the gospel
of prosperity.

Trigger warnings liberal
on many texts,
conservative on the triggers
of the armament amassed
in the closet.

Within a Fortnite
of independent study,
respect for human life
was virtually ingrained.

No public school cliques,
yet something clicked:
he packed compassionate nihilism
at high capacity,
packaged weirdness too explosive
for Austin or within
any city limits.

Smear the queer,

we called it,
or black man tackle,
so smear your derision
full upon us
though we didn't have a clue
who a queer was
and what would a black man
want with a town like ours:
segregation in spades?
like the ball carrier
gazelling away
pack giving chase
grabbing
clawing
surrounding
closing in
sensing weakness
piling on
bodies heaving
breath and sweat mingling
inflicting pain
giggling
queer practice, indeed
behind the wood shop
100 yards or so
from where the high school boys

engaged in more uniform brutality
save for the Friday night
I was sidelined
tied and straitjacketed
for the homecoming pageantry
next to a kindergarten princess on the dais
wailing to be unleashed
my mentality back with the mob
instincts more spit than polish
in the first of many lessons
of how easily we dress it up
and the muscle required
to conceal the memory that twitches
fast, then slow.

Queue

Noun and verb,
I've loved you both,
your elementary Darwinism:
the first shall be first.
Sweet line, I've held you,
toed you,
read between you,
stayed within you,
and yes, I've occasionally
gotten you crossed,
drawn you in sand,
even felt I'd come
to the end of you,
but I'd never been cut,
not deeply, until now.

You let someone
come between us
while I was at the jukebox
playing some Buck Owens
for my dad.
Who knew that hipster with the iPhone
was your type?
Then at *our* restaurant,
that drone from the suburbs
with a Nowait app.

Really? Your grounds for ending
our solid relationship
is the instant gratification
of these children's
fragmented attention?

Do you want to see me fall apart,
because that is virtually assured
as fault lines open
between every vibrating atom
of my being
and I slip
out of time and joint,
the unmissed link
in the newly dissembled
evolutionary line.

Conversion

Like a test run
for the rapture,
St. Bede's Catholic Church
in Kelly, Kansas towers
over all buildings of commerce
no longer in existence.

Next highest rises
the pitching mound
of the neighboring field
testifying to the transcendent
power of sport.

In my ninth year,
I faced a hometown pitcher
possessed of the spirit
of the game
but too reliant on faith
without works
to control his fervor.

Three times
I stepped into the batter's box,
three times he delivered unto me
the power and the glory

transubstantiated
and a trinity of bruises
on my flesh like rosaries.

The fourth time I entered
as if into a confessional
where my Methodist
prayers unrote
had no power to stay the scourge
I embraced
for sins of which I knew not
yet
by the time I rose
from my knees
I was converted
to eternal spectator.

Scope

We live
one moment
to the next
'til G-forces cause
memory
to flex.
Decades of spinning
scatter recollection
equal parts tragedy
equal parts protection.
The present
a past
the future
a hope:
God is teaching
scope.

The ice cream man drives way too fast
down my street

and the bass from his speakers
drowns out the treble chime.
He's blowing through stop signs
and the hours by which he's salaried,
this skinny should-be-post-
adolescent
keeping the driving beat
with Kendrick or Kanye,
loath to leave a spot
where cellphone serves as seat belt,
not that we'd want to see him stand:
striped Bomb Pop in one hand,
pants sagging near the low water mark
of striped boxers
in the other

so unlike the fat man
from my youth,
cheery though the beads of sweat
pooled atop his cherry cheeks,
circumventing the van a waddling truth
in advertising,
setting the bait on the shore
of the park,

then trolling in a widening circle
for the elusive catch
of gamey ones
flushed from thick reeds and rushes
and depths of imagination,
such pains to garner attention
from a multitude less divided

than in this palely reflected world
of factory-fed juveniles
who by the time they school consensus
of who iWant as friend to follow
to emerge from aquarium lit basements
in genetically engineered glow
can but blink as they surface
into some wake of what they don't even know
they have missed.

Asian Markets

One night in Bangkok,
I was naïve enough
to be amazed
that my friend James
found a girlfriend
in less than 12 hours.
She was petite, sexy, witty,
and her laughter lifted like a songbird
after each of his jokes.
My envy swelled
as she would hang on him
as if increase in appetite had grown
by what it fed on.

It wasn't until I inquired
about a friend for me
that James confessed:
I'd been without a woman
the past three years,
so upon arrival in Thailand,
I visited a massage parlor.
He paid her by the day,
and yes, indeed, she knew someone
eager to meet
another handsome American.

Somchai was better than advertised,
and she matter-of-factly stated
that dating for salary
was simply an internship
while she saved for business school.
She opened her portfolio
of her international investments
in a Japanese boyfriend,
Chinese boyfriend, French boyfriend…
She took my trembling hand
and turned the pages,
presenting pictures of pleased associates,
pointing out her assets,
increasing my interest,
bullish that her stock
was rising.

Sum of Our Parts

The artificial is still
striking to see:
a hook where a hand
ought to be,
prosthetics
from the knees down,
myoelectric currents
phantom feel for the ground.

Is this the better surrender
shedding the corporeal this way:
epiphany of the void sans
meditation on decay?

Fragmented reconnaissance missions
preparing the way for the soul,
flesh touches the hem of the captain then
rendezvous with the whole.

Faith by Works

*If I come back
as an animal,
I hope it's a bull,*
and he knew
from whence he spoke
owning as many as 150
at one point
for dissemination
amongst local farmers
for $250 a breeding season.

Dad never was a true believer in the word
of others
shunning stock registration papers
preferring instead to cultivate
a cross section of crossbreeds,
variety to satisfy
any renter's needs.
Simmental, Angus, Limousin,
would bellow and fight
upon return of an expat,
tearing through barbed wire
and hedge posts
as a Hereford once did
penetrating the sanctuary
of a fellow farmer
so proud of his picture-
perfect purebred Angus herd,
black strokes on green canvas.

Love thy neighbor
though he threatened litigation
until his epiphany
at the Falls City Sale Barn
where the black white face
black sheep calves
sold seventeen cents a pound higher
than the pedigreed Angus.
Thus was Art Kramer converted,
renting a Hereford
the next year,
leaving Dad to proselytize
to the next neighbor

as he hauled his creatures
to foreign pastures,
witnessing the purebred instincts
in the way they sniffed the cows,
mounted indiscriminately
the way God intended
and Dad had judged
they would
before driving away
down the dirt road,
his faith renewed
by this earth's mere
miraculous works.

Grade Inflation

My wife's son
proudly accessed for us
his perfect 4.0 report card:
two A's, a B, two C's.
Weighted honors courses,
he explained,
and extra credit.
If Mrs. Harris was fair,
I'd've had a 4.2
which made me want to reevaluate
a lifetime's worth of core curriculum:

that relationship I swore I failed -
could that not be reclassified
as a master's course in psychology,
with the added credit that majoring in
manic depression required?

those times self-interest
made me an average son, at best,
need I the reminder
that my instructors graded on a curve?

but mostly it motivated me
to enroll in this new school
of soft knocks,

build up some extra credit
with the boss
and the wife,
reassured me that in the final judgment
I'll be given a pass
now that I've dedicated myself
to giving 110%
for the sum
of my remainder.

The Mendoza Line

Full disclosure:
I was scared of the ball
in little league,
so they stuck me with the clovers
out in right field
which may account
for my bias
towards our hometown right fielder
who just won millions in arbitration
for batting a shade above the Mendoza line.
He sports a gold glove,
granted,
but he succeeds one fifth of the time
against pitchers with ERAs
like hot air balloons.

So can I plead precedent
when applying to the president
for an achievement award
if my standards hold
that it's common
that a core of four
of five students
in this ADD-juiced era
will be left behind
upon occasion?

Statisticians don't care
whether Mario divorced or not,
but before my wife and I slug it out again,
metaphorically speaking,
I'll work the count
of times I compliment,
single her out
for attention,
double my efforts
at empathy
one out of every four days,
so our combined average
stays fair of .500,
the American League norm,
our Mendoza line in the sand.

Cottonwood

I bounded off the pencil yellow bus
for the last time in months
as its leaves glistened a greeting
and flurries flew past my face
to drift by driveway's edge:
Happy New Year!
and auld acquaintance
already forgot.

Roots like toppled columns
traveled parallel to the ground
before divining moisture,
diving to the depths:
conduits to the cool current
of the creek
and a blond boy's bastion
where nine months of lessons
could lay siege
in futility.

Late one summer
at the edge of manhood,
I watched with Dad
from the living room window
as one of those regal storms
of the plains

announced its presence
with bombastic flourish.
My noble tree
bowed in supplication
before being knighted
by lightning's sword
in a crown of purple.

No words were spoken,
but as Dad turned away,
I knew that all things desiccate,
combust, or decay,
thus while one may
drink deep and keep
the blaze or burn at bay.

Nondenominational

For he gives his sunlight to both the evil and the good,
and he sends rain on the just and the unjust alike.
- Matthew 5:45

Two seasons in Vietnam:
Swelter and Rainy.

Six months of the latter
impede no local
awash in his capital
ideas.
When the heavens open,
bicycles and motorbikes
transporting timber,
poultry,
or families of five
pull briefly
to the side of the street
where plastic ponchos are donned
before the pilot
pushes off
into the ankle-deep flow,
navigating through the flood
of traffic.

No umbrellas obtrude
on the crowded sidewalks
save one of a wandering expat
unimmersed
in the beauty of this baptism
of the just
and unjust
alike.

Flint Hills

In the Flint Hills,
I spent a couple of nights
in a pasture with an Angus bull,
camping next to a valley pond
to which he'd descend from the ridge
for a drink
while sizing up
his strange companion.

At night,
his Johnny Cash bass
through the prairie wind
rattled me to my bones.

Just me and this old bull
bellowing
for everything missing.

Friends of the Truth

n Adults who attend Apostolic Christian Church services, but who have yet to make the commitments necessary for membership.

1.

The Apostolic Christians
deemed it contrary to God's will
for cattle to be dehorned.
After a gory battle
between bulls
and another between
hay feeder and bull,
the animal twisting
its captive head
until its neck broke,
Great-grandpa Simon
believed God's plan
could be improved upon,
so he took the bull by the horns
and dehorned his herd.
The brothers of the Church
preached a scathing admonishment
from the bully pulpit,
so the subsequent Sunday,
a holy day of rest,
Simon led his wife and children to work
in the field nearest the country road

where all the brethren drove
on the way to worship
so they could witness the power
and the glory
of one prideful German farmer.

2.

God's creation contains
abundant pleasure in gratis
so that one should not pay
for any type of entertainment.
Grandpa John was out of tune
with this doctrine,
purchasing a piano so his daughters
could learn to play.
The brothers paid a visit
and told him to get rid of it,
John playing the devil's advocate
all the while.
The brothers communed
in a corner, emerging with the compromise
that John move the piano
out of the family room and upstairs.
Brothers, John commanded,
if you want that piano upstairs,
move it yourselves!
The piano stayed,

foundation upon which
John built his defiance,
wearing out the seat
of his trousers
as he biked to a church
in a neighboring state.

3.

Some people need more churchin'
than others
was the refrain of my father's favorite
homemade hymn,
composed shortly after two older siblings
foolishly robbed a bank
during the Great Depression.
The AC kids were merciless
in their taunts
and their playground beatings,
a *Do unto others*
offering no sanctuary
from the turmoil at home,
so Joe stayed afield
eventually singing his hymns
in his own fields
Sunday mornings
the rest of his life.

4.

The rift was far less dramatic for me,
just wide enough to stir
my anti-authoritarian blood.
Two of the 10 girls in my class,
one fifth of our dating opportunities
(had my crippling shyness not already rendered
that an unlikely possibility),
joined the Church
summer before freshman year.
They stopped playing sports,
attending dances,
engaging in sophomoric debate.
Their hair went up in buns,
symbolic of the higher plane they trod
than the rest of us
in the same high school halls.
It wasn't their fault.
These children were instructed
how to behave around the masses,
when to deign,
when to withdraw,
but such was the transformative power
of the commitment
that even witnesses such as I
were altered.
From then on,
I was simply a friend of the truth,
never again to be mistaken
for the real thing.

Irony

They tore down the vertigo-inducing ladder
with the narrow steps
to the sheet metal slide,
screws and bolts jiggling loose,
snagging skin in gentle reminder
to mind the middle way,

likewise the teeter-totter
with the splintered board
and the merry-go-round
capable of breakneck speeds
inches above the rocky gravel

no doubt to avoid
the shock of a litigious slap
and the concussive effects
of a bruising courtroom battle
in this era of strained community ties
and fractured personal responsibility

but the vision that took root
over coffee in air conditioned construction offices
also included the removal of all
the old-growth maple, ash and oak

so even if today's kid
pulled out the earbuds and put down the device,
convinced Mom or Brad to chaperone
and overcame a deficit
of attention
to surmount the privacy fence,

the heat bouncing off
the all-weather mulch,
monkey bar burns
and the scalding from a slide
of suburban beige plastic
would dissuade the most calloused
of country rednecks
and hardened city vagrants
that nostalgia from the deepest recesses
of my memory
could offer up.

Cold Case
(after Sorescu)

Pencils in hand,
the investigators scramble in,
scouring the scene,
examining the fallen body

making note of the wounds
of unrequited love,
points of impact
for doubt and fear,
shocks to the system
of sudden absences

recording evidence
of how he fought back
with music
literature
procreation

worst suspicions confirmed,
pinpointing the exact moment
he must have caught
his first throe of death:
time of birth.

Parochial Praise

Can you expect them
to be observant?
You're the bellhop in this scene,
subservient.

A liberal education
failed to give you clarity
regarding natural selection and the gospel
of prosperity.

Up front with your *Hamlet*
and existential musings —
for a tiny percentage
life is not so confusing.

They've already decided
this is where it's at.
Parents and their right wing representatives
are eager to vouch for that.

Born on third,
think they tripled with autonomy.
Their blessings will trickle down,
stimulate the team's economy

while the mothers defy time's ravages
with a nip, tan, and tuck
modestly buzzed to make the basement lists
of Moms I'd Like to Fuck.

Alpha begets Alpha;
the blond leads the blonde
marching toward glorious Omega
uniformly on and on.

What comfort to already
be among the chosen ones
sequestered in a slice of heaven —
St. Peter's work all done.

Slough

Loud enough to wake the dead
my wife will whisper in the dark,
yet amphitheater shells at dawn:
a spectre chorus clutching bark.

Underground as nymphs
17 years long
before bursting into light
and company and song.

I hope to raise
but half that din
time it comes
to shed my skin.

Relative Cold Front

A family recipe
for coping with August swelter
in an old farmhouse
without air conditioning:

Step one:
Step outside for the morning,
afternoon, and evening.
Throw rectangular bales
of clover or alfalfa
onto a moving wagon
or stack them ten high.
Just try to keep up
with your old man.
Rest in the shade
of the loft
while catching hay
coming off the conveyer.

Step two:
At sunset,
walk to the house
as the temperature drops
three degrees.
Peel off wet jeans
and long sleeved western shirt.

Take the most well-deserved shower
of your life
or settle for a patriarch's sink cleanse,
hand-to-hand combat
with washcloth, Lava, and towel.

Step three:
Turn on the box fan
in the window inches from your bed.
Lie naked in the dark night
as muscles gratefully release
their tension.
Feel the goose bumps rise
on your flesh.
Pull up the sheet,
ward off the chill.

Angels and Devils

God must've needed another angel
thus we instruct our teachers
to mark them absent forever,
God must've needed another angel
patron saints to reconcile us
to the unalienable wits we've severed,
God must've needed another angel
so Saint Peter's capacity for browsing
his magazines increases in clip,
God must've needed another angel
and from Darwin's chalice
the literalists in rapture sip,
God must've needed another angel
as if we think the playing field
will level,
God must've needed another angel
while down here we could use
fewer of these devils.

Best case scenario

the periodontist said,
we save the tooth
by grafting bits of cadaver bone
into the hole above it.
Then she left me
to stare out the window
into the sunshine
as I told myself
not to be so melodramatic
considering what diagnoses
were being delivered
this same moment
in antiseptic rooms
all over the world
while I'd be home
in a couple hours
joking with my wife
about giving her
my dying kiss
but to major in English
is to major in death
according to Billy Collins,
so I can't help but attempt to calculate
what percentage cadaver
I already am

while meditating
on the number of similar windows
through which I'll squint
into my golden years
best case scenario.

Stockyards

His legs young oaks
Dad rooted near the endgate
should sow or barrow break
in desperate dash toward self-preservation.
The trailer grunted and groaned
while he changed into go-to-town
Osh Kosh overalls,
donned a cleaner cowboy hat
to set off in the company of 61 Country
and a copilot with an exaggerated sense
of importance.

After unloading at Swift and Henry,
he'd query, *Do you want to stay in the nice motel
or the crummy hotel?*
though he knew the only answer
that fired a nine-year-old's imagination:
the grand lobby in ancient opulence,
accordion elevator gates
sung shut by an old Italian
who raised us fitfully to unprecedented heights
of the sixth floor
where I'd gaze out the window
at the pens teeming with life
so close to death.

Now not even a stock postcard
is to be found in the tourist traps
along Michigan Avenue.
Oh, Chicago,
hog butcher for the world,
has your past dissolved like my memory
of those lines learned
in Mrs. Miller's fourth grade classroom?
Where is that boy,
right-hand man to the last real cowboy behind the wheel,
getting a wink from the old Italian
before falling asleep with no delusions
that any of this grandeur
would ever end?

Graveyard in Passing

White wicker crosses
always take me by surprise,
breaks in my windshield
cracking the continuity
of my placid horizon.

These thin, fragile planks
draped in wreaths
of weathered plastic,
forget-me-nots slipping
slowly from the shoulders
of a shrugging world.

Erected hurriedly by a heartbroken matriarch
self-conscious in her solitary service?
Or did she linger
in her roadside prayer
turning defiantly to the speeding traffic,
unwiped tears in her eyes?

Cruising at 90 through life,
teenagers race past any thoughts
of dying in sleep and peace
at 90, grandchildren draped
uncomfortably in neckties.

So, instead of granite headstones,
this white wicker whipping in the wind.
Instead of solid stone sanctuary,
pebbles spewed by rubber on asphalt.
Instead of a slow train of mourners,
glimpses from the quick.

Diaspora

Noble manors,
storied frames set majestically
back from gravel roads,
once sharing a section
with two or three sovereign fiefdoms.

Now epidermis peels
to bone,
narrow driveways cede
to sunflower,
pigweed,
cocklebur —
encroaching armies unchecked
at the border.

An honorable tribe
dispersed to the lighted corners
of the world.
Marrying for love
not practicality,
regenerating in luxury
not necessity,
increasing yields
in vague dissatisfaction,
gleaning wisdom
from soil less fertile.

House of Cards

For the fortunate few,
the deal is enough
though most resort
to bluff,
and if luck of the draw
lands some on the street,
may pardon be granted
if a hand tends to cheat.
With pleasure for some
in pain others play,
some trump the odds
to hold fate at bay.
With desperate devils
or one of their gods,
most cut a deal
to better the odds.

Bid and bet
but all the while
the jesters smile
at all your guile,
and the royal flush
once almost seen
in limits high
and fields of green,

now turncoat jacks
and fickle queens.
And bloat kings
once so proud,
severe,
in profile now
tell thin
and sere.

Danse Macabre

During Japan's summer Obon Festival,
spirits of the dead are greeted
upon their return.
Houses and graves are swept,
and food or cigarette or sake offerings
are placed upon alters
as descendants dance
to welcome ancestors home.

So summon your credulity:
go to the grave
of your father
on the most sweltering
of August afternoons.
Clip the grass,
hoe the weeds,
aerate the soil.
In his memory,
work up
the most unclouded sweat
of your life,
then lay down
and let it roll
in salty rivulets
to the thirsty earth.

Let the marble
cool your temples
as you recall
your common name.

Present your offerings
devoutly.
Do you remember
what epicurean sensations
stirred his soul
when he was corporeal?
Pray you've chosen wisely:
this dance is for you,
purely for you.

Parent-Teacher Conferences

The first sits across from me
talking of traffic, weather, sports,
fidgeting in his chair
before finally mentioning his son's ADHD struggles.
I glance over the grades,
begin to ask how I can best help his child succeed,
but he's spotted a buddy to greet
across the commons,
then proceeds to change the subject.

I'm concerned about your daughter,
I say to the next, tactfully as possible.
She spends much of class flirting,
and boys distract her from the tasks at hand.
She purrs and brushes my hand with hers,
freshly tanned save for a white band
on the third finger.
Perhaps we should discuss this in more detail.
Let me give you my personal e-mail:
hotmom69@gmail.com.

We're really at wit's end,
the nice couple complains.
We've encouraged him to cut back on the computer,
pleaded with him to limit the video games,

begged him to moderate texting time.
Have you any suggestions
to instill some discipline?

I walk out into the crisp October evening
immersed in the pedagogy
of empathy,
thanking God in his heaven
for instilling order
in a sometimes confusing world.

Forgiving Eve

'Twas not a matter
of temptation,
gullibility,
preoccupation.
She *saw* the apple
of creation
saw the worm
in penetration,
formed a feminine
revelation:
an epiphany of
recuperation.

Beheld a beast
but in potential
a fellow mortal
forced to crawl
divine
before the fall,
offered faith that would forestall
damnation:
acceptance of the gall,
redemption through esteem
salvation for us all.

Aunt Priscilla

The mulberries heralded
your return,
passion purple by early June
when I'd see your Caravan
kicking up dust on the driveway
to the last station of the pilgrimage
to your Kansas homeland.
We'd ascend to the Mount
to pick and pontificate
while your voice cried
in the wilderness:
The dumb will inherit the earth!
wisdom gleaned
from another long year
in the elementary classroom,
and I'd laugh —
prophets are ever misunderstood
in their native land.

You'd speak of transgression,
how Grandpa would beat the fear of man
into my father
whose purity prevented those sins
revisitation rights;
of resurrection,

when you were dragged by a stirrup
across the cloddy earth
from which Grandma raised you
and anointed your bruises.

Forty years you spent tested
in the Barstow desert
driving snakes from the schoolyard
with a baseball bat
and bringing back the rattles for show and tell
all the while plotting
your return to the Father.
The stone's bought and rolled into place
you'd chuckle
and still you rise from your seat
at the right hand of memory
rock of my ages
upon which I build
my church.

Parental Prayer

Treat those you love
with care.
To follow your dreams,
we pray you'll dare.

Fertile imagination,
respect for all creation,
unsullied reputation -

such virtues are a plus,
but not for the sake of God
please, simply please
outlive us.

Communion

A cracker box gym, the old man called it,
as my team trotted out for pregame warmups
taking the tiny court more suited for its principle purpose
as lunchroom at Saints Peter and Paul Junior High School.

Short stacks three bleachers low crowded close
forcing folks in front to shift legs on inbounds plays.
The top of each key overlapped the midcourt circle
demanding a ¾ court advance to break the suffocating press
before our guards could mercifully retreat to the midline
to set the offense and our shaken confidence.

The introduction of players rang as familiar to hometown fans
as the Litany of the Saints:
Holthaus, Sudbeck, Broxterman, Rottinghaus, Schmitz
sprouted like lowland crops from fertile farmland families
regenerating with the growing seasons.

These same names pealed
across the Knights of Columbus parking lot
throughout my high school Saturday nights.
Manchildren downed Bud Light around a communal keg
until epiphany brought proclamation that mass began
in a few hours, and a joyful processional
weaved its way towards parked pickups.

I'd attempt in vain to summon an image of them
crouched in humble supplication,
knees and elbows bent in the stasis of prayer,
in full passivity of the responsorial psalm,
fostering a healthy fear of mortal failings.

I could only behold them at full hubristic height,
a blur of lanky limbs obscuring the hardwood
impenitently enticing the opposition into a half court trap,
denying entry passes as Father Michael would urge them
to deny sin,
transubstantiated, in perfect communion,
possessing utter certainty that their covenant promised
not only the one true path to His Kingdom,
but also divine right to victory
in the sanctuary of home court.

Talking About the Weather

A finger raised from the wheel
of the Ford or Chevy truck,
chin lifted in small salute
of the common journeys
down these dusty gravel roads.
Passerby, these are greetings
from a reticent folk
who commune, if at all,
over coffee at the cafe
comforted by the harmony
of their stilted hymn
in metaphor:
Looks like rain
that falls on both the just and the unjust
from time to time.
Bad stretch we've been havin'
but this, too, shall pass
if we persevere.
Nice day, isn't it?
then may the Lord continue
to show you his mercy.
I'm burning daylight
and may your labor bear fruit
for you and yours
until we meet again.

Boyd Bauman grew up on a small ranch south of the town of Bern, Kansas (population 200). His dad was a storyteller and his mom the family scribe. Grist for the mill included stints as a flight attendant out of New York City, dude ranch worker and ski bum in Colorado, and King Salmon fisherman in Alaska. Boyd has taught English in Hiroshima, Japan and Saigon, Vietnam. He is currently a librarian and writer in the Kansas City area. Boyd lives with his lovely wife Lisa and their little poets Haven and Milly. Visit him at boydbauman.weebly.com.

www.ingramcontent.com/pod-product-compliance
Lightning Source LLC
Chambersburg PA
CBHW020126130526
44591CB00032B/539